RETIRE YOUNG, RETIRE RICH FROM BUSINESS OPPORTUNITIES

Discover The Most Prominent Business Opportunities And Methods In The 80's, 90's And 21st Century

Terms and Conditions

LEGAL NOTICE

The Publisher has strived to be as accurate and complete as possible in the creation of this report, notwithstanding the fact that he does not warrant or represent at any time that the contents within are accurate due to the rapidly changing nature of the Internet.

While all attempts have been made to verify information provided in this publication, the Publisher assumes no responsibility for errors, omissions, or contrary interpretation of the subject matter herein. Any perceived slights of specific persons, peoples, or organizations are unintentional.

In practical advice books, like anything else in life, there are no guarantees of income made. Readers are cautioned to reply on their own judgment about their individual circumstances to act accordingly.

This book is not intended for use as a source of legal, business, accounting or financial advice. All readers are advised to seek services of competent professionals in legal, business, accounting and finance fields.

You are encouraged to print this book for easy reading.

Table Of Contents

Forward

Chapter 1:
About How We Think

Chapter 2:
Moving Into The New Era

Chapter 3:
What We Can Learn From The Big Dogs

Chapter 4:
Entrepreneurial Vision

Chapter 5:
Going Green

Chapter 6:
Why You Must Look For Alternatives

Chapter 7:
Take Control

Wrapping Up

Foreword

Surveys bring out that most individuals would like to retire young—fifty-five or younger—and many would choose their thirties or forties if they could. However can they? Absolutely. And so may you!

It's going to take more than would-be thinking, however; it's likewise going to take a sufficient net worth and a few effective strategies. The more cash you earn, the easier it ought to be to retire young. But, irrespective of income, here is your guide to exiting the workforce early: spend less, save more, and invest wisely. Sound easy enough?

Then put it into practice. By following that easy advice you are able to take control of your future, retire young, and begin enjoying what ought to be the best years of your life. If you aren't already well on your way, though, it's crucial that you begin now.

Retire Young, Retire Rich From Business Opportunities

Discover The Most Prominent Business Opportunities And Methods In The 80's, 90's And 21st Century.

Chapter 1:
About How We Think

Synopsis

Cash flow is the most crucial word in the world of revenue. The second most crucial word is leverage. Leverage is the cause some individuals become wealthy and other people don't become wealthy. The reason less that five percent of all Americans are rich is because only five percent understand how to utilize the power of leverage.

Among the recognized forms of leverage is the leverage of borrowing cash. Millions of individuals scramble financially because the power of debt leverage is utilized against them. Great debt makes you wealthy and bad debt makes you poor.

The most potent sort of leverage in the world, your brain, has the might to make you wealthy or make you poor.

Beliefs

Wealthy individuals utilize rich words and poor individuals utilize poor words. Your mind may be your most powerful asset or it may be your most powerful liability.

The difference between wealthy individuals and poor individuals is that poor individuals state "I can't afford it" more often that wealthy individuals. If you wish to retire young and retire rich, you'll have to utilize your mind in your favor, not against you.

Forbes magazine specifies rich as $1 million or more a year in revenue. The issue with having a job is that it gets in the way of getting wealthy.

Most individuals have a plan to be poor. That's why so many individuals state, "When I retire, my revenue will go down." Put differently, they're stating, "I plan of working hard all my life and then I'll become poorer after I retire".

Millions of workers are today counting on their pension plan, plans like 401(k) and IRA. Employees are now responsible for their retirement. In the Industrial Age, it was the company or the government that would mind of your financial needs once your workdays were over.

There's one tragic flaw in these Information Age pension plans. The flaw is that most of these plans are indexed to the stock exchange, and as you might have noticed, stock exchanges go up and stock exchanges crash.

Projecting to work hard all your life is a poor plan. For a lot of baby boomers, time, our most crucial asset, is running out.

In real life less than five percent of the U.S. population is wealthy because ninety-five percent of the population might want to be rich but only five percent takes action.

The three main assets that make individuals wealthy and let them retire young:

1. Real property
2. Paper assets
3. Businesses

Retiring young and rich requires spending time acquiring assets instead of working for money.

This book is written to help you in discovering your own financial freedom…freedom from the drudgery of just getting by.

Poor individuals utilize poor words and poor words produce poor individuals. If you are able to change your words and your thoughts to those of the wealthy, retiring young and retiring wealthy will be simple.

We all have questions. The difference is what we do with those questions.

The greatest challenge you have is to challenge your own self-distrust and your laziness. It's your self-distrust and your laziness that specifies and limit who you are. If you wish to change what you are, you have to take on you self-distrust and you laziness. It's your self-distrust and laziness that keep you small. It's you self-distrust and laziness that deny you the life you wish.

There's no one in your way except you and your doubts about you. It's simple to stay the same. It's simple not to change. Most individuals choose to stay the same all their lives. If you'll take on your self-distrust and your laziness, you'll discover the door to your freedom.

The reason many individuals don't do what they can do is because they don't have a strong enough "why". Once you find the" why", it is simple to find you own "how to" to riches. Rather than looking inside of themselves to discover their own "why" they wish to become wealthy, most individuals look for the easy road to wealth, and the issue with the easy road is that the easy road commonly ends in a dead end.

3 more paths to great riches are:

1. Bettering business skills
2. Bettering money management skills
3. Bettering investment skills

If you discover yourself arguing with a great idea, you might want to quit arguing. Whenever somebody states something like 'I can't afford it' or 'I can't do it' to something they wish, they've a large problem. Why in the world would somebody state, "I can't afford it' or 'I can't do it' to something they wish? I was arguing because I was protecting myself from the pain that dreaming big dreams may bring if that big dream doesn't become a reality. I had dreamed and bombed. I realized that I was arguing against failing again, not against the aspiration.

A hint: I learned years ago that passion is a combination of love and detest. Unless somebody has a passion for something, it's hard to achieve anything. If you want something, be passionate. Passion provides energy to your life.

If you wish something you don't have, discover why you love what you want and why you detest not having what you want. When you combine those two thoughts, you'll discover the energy to get off your seat and go get anything you require.

I've heard many individuals state, "Money doesn't make you happy". That statement has some truth to it. But what cash does do is buy me the time to do what I love and pay others to do what I detest doing.

How many of you plan on retiring early?" "How many of you would like to retire in your 40s and be financially free for the rest of your life?

Chapter 2:
Moving Into The New Era

Synopsis

Nobody succeeded in 2010 by attempting to save his or her way to prosperity! As we enter this decade, its crucial business leaders recognize the only way to produce a strong profit is to have a strong revenue. Some recommendations:

A New View

Go to where the growth is, and where you are able to bring in revenue. Don't chase after just any business; chase the business where you are able to fruitfully grow. Be choosy to invest resources in growth markets.

Center efforts on markets you understand best. It's crucial you comprehend not to do merely what you like, but learn to do what buyers appreciate.

Release junk, customs and "playing it safe" behaviors. Growth is all about learning to do what the market desires, not attempting to protect the past – whether actions, products or even buyers.

You can't grow unless you're willing to learn from everything around you. Those who flourish don't quit – they seek ways to turn those sour experiences into suitable ones. What is your willingness to learn from the market?

Efficiency is the greatest obstacle to innovation. You don't have to be extravagant to succeed, but you can't be a miser investing in only the matters you know, and have done previously.

We don't learn if we don't share. Developing insight from the environment occurs when all inputs are shared, and lots of individuals contribute to the process.

There's more to success than the ability of positive thinking, but it's really hard to gain insight and push innovation when you are a pessimist. Growth is a chance to learn, and accomplish exciting things. That ought to be a positive for everyone. Remember, we don't fear change, we fear the unidentified. As your experiences teach you about fresh opportunities and markets your fear will lessen and exhilaration will replace it.

Recognizing that you can't beat the cost-cutting horse eternally, it's time business leaders recognize that we've been under-investing in conception for the last decade. While GM, Circuit City, Blockbuster, have been failing, Apple, Google, Facebook and Twitter have held double-digit growth! Those who keep innovating recognize that markets aren't dead, they're scarcely shifting!

Growth is there for businesses willing to innovate fresh answers that attract buyers – and their dollars! For each dead DVD store there's someone making cash streaming downloads. Businesses merely have to invest more in innovation and less on efficiency and "core" plans.

Work harder at trying to "connect the dots". Pick up on weak signals, before other people, and establish scenarios to comprehend the future affect of these signals as they get stronger. For instance, the net predicts that greater utilization of mobile devices will annihilate some businesses. But for each of these there will be a big number of fresh business opportunities emerging. Simply view the efforts of Foursquare and Groupon to see where emergence businesses are headed.

Pay attention to what's happening in the world, and consider what it means for your business. Oil has an affect; what opportunity does it produce? Slumping network TV watching has an affect – how will you leverage this tilt? Don't simply wander through your market, responding to events using auto-pilot. Work out what fresh trends are developing, and learn to realize growth opportunities. Utilize market events to be proactive.

It takes lots of trial and learning – and that means the willingness to experiment. Very much. Plan on experimenting. Invest in it. And then plan on the favorable results.

Continue asking "why". Then, produce scenarios and ask "why not". Markets won't tell you what the next huge thing is, but if you ask a lot of questions your scenarios about the future will be a whole lot better – and your experiment will be significantly more productive.

You can't cast your net too wide in the effort to receive multiple viewpoints. Nothing is narrower than our own convictions. Only by actively tapping input from wide-ranging sources may we develop alternative solutions that have greater value.

We get so comfortable talking to the same individuals, inside our companies and outside, that we don't realize how much we hear only supports our biases. Develop, and expand, your network as fast as conceivable.

Chapter 3:
What We Can Learn From The Big Dogs

Synopsis

A lot of the early dot-coms spotted the excellent opportunities the net offered and sought to sow those seeds of momentous opportunity. But one company leaps out, even today, above them all: Amazon.com.

This company foresaw crisis and managed change to see on the far side the obvious channels of business to what the internet may mean for global commerce. Its vision was so sharp it went on to become the world's number 1 net retailer—a title it still holds now.

The original net book retailer now dominates class after class of net sales. The story of how this company started, and how it made the transition from specialty store to net super-site, is one of repeated application of one feature in particular that personifies the position of business leaders: circular vision.

A Lesson

Amazon.com is inextricably linked to its founder, Jeff Bezos. By the time he was 30 years old, Bezos had started to center on the net. There he spotted a huge opportunity during a time when the net was predominantly utilized by academics and federal agencies. Seeing beyond the obvious to potential commercial diligences, he saw a jumbo opportunity in the general public's growing usage of the net.

He focused in further on this source of opportunity through research. He looked first at the top twenty mail-order businesses in the U.S. with the intention of determining which ones may be made more effective through the use of the net.

Books, Bezos soon ascertained, were ideal. The cataloging demands and expense made their sale unprofitable for mail order. On the net, the expense was chiefly opportunity cost. A hurriedly arranged trip to the American Booksellers Convention in LA further convinced him of the viability of selling books by the net. There he distinguished that the industry's major players already had electronic lists of their products. All he needed to do was amass those lists in a central location where they could be searched and ordered by the public.

He gave up his lucrative Greater New York job and its promising future. It was simply days later when he typed a business plan on his laptop.

It has been stated that he made his decision based on a view of reviewing life from its end to imagine the results. Though he possibly didn't describe it per se, he was actively applying circular vision. He was expecting the future, looking around and beyond the obvious tracts of his time.

Nowadays he and his company reap the ceaseless harvest of that original broadened observation. It's perhaps no happenstance that the company's name, Amazon, is attached to circular vision. Named after the long and curving river with seemingly infinite tributaries, Amazon.com is the ever-flowing, ever-changing nature of opportunity.

And the company has held to this dynamic. Its early operation represented what would later become the criterion of the net start-up. Bezos established shop in a house. Utilizing limited capital raised from kinsperson and acquaintances, he designed, built, and tried out the beta-version site. After a successful month of testing, and almost precisely a year later, Amazon.com was at last launched to the public.

The only marketing was buzz, and that was all it took. In thirty days, Amazon.com had sold books into all 50 states and 45 countries beyond. By 1995, Amazon.com realized its first hundred order day and was doing more than $20,000 in sales monthly.

But it wasn't simply this early success, fueled by early perceptivity into e-commerce, that provided good fortune. He anticipated the coming wave like almost no one else. He saw that the net would grow quickly. Perhaps most cannily, he saw the potential to transform the net into something that would alter the way that individuals did business forever. He thus centered his company's energy on riding the swell as fast and as far as it would take them.

Sensing from the start that books were simply an entry into the net market, Bezos began to leadAmazon.com into additional sales arenas. He didn't aspire to be "Earth's greatest bookstore" but instead "Earth's greatest anything store." In 97, he added CDs and movies, and by 98, Amazon.com featured five more classes in its product line: software, electronics, video games, playthings, and home improvement.

Not everything tried has worked, but his good fortune has continued all the same. This is the effect of sowing one great seed of opportunity.

 The six features of perspective on business leaders:

Amazon delivers its cultural perspective by looking to determine fresh ways to continuously reinvent itself. Nowadays, Amazon is known even as much for its Kindle e-reader devices as it's known for its net store.

As noted, Bezos predicted crisis and managed changed in the book industry. He saw the potential for net commerce before almost anybody. He produced the net book retailing industry and he continues to see opportunities other people don't.

Bezos' leap of faith let him produce possibilities that he aimed to share with other people. His passionate pursuits to produce fresh standards of excellence might not have always led to good luck, but he utilized the lessons of those rare failures to re-craft Amazon's scheme to their eventual greater success.

Since his early days, Bezos' entrepreneurial spirit has always stayed alive. Intrinsically, Amazon's innovations remain endless.
Amazon's story is one that's embedded in sharing the harvest of one's success with other people. Not only did Amazon share their mighty ecommerce platform with others retailers, they let independent authors who didn't have the means to promote, market and sell their books – have instant access to a channel of distribution with global reach.

The Amazon culture powerfully embraces the idea that making errors are an essential part of questing after fresh ideas. At Amazon, everybody is encouraged to have a brave attitude towards experimentation and the future. This attitude is imperative to Amazon's ongoing success; without it, innovation would shrivel and die.

Amazon excels among Internet companies in a lot of ways, but the most crucial is that it's thrived by fully living the entrepreneurial attitude with which it began. As long as Amazon keeps that entrepreneurial spirit alive, I may confidently predict that they'll stay at the forefront of retail – and Internet – innovation. You can learn a great lesson from them.

Chapter 4:
Entrepreneurial Vision

Synopsis

Finding an entrepreneurial idea is simple if you have vision. When you view an industry, you are able to see opportunity, needed change or simply individuals putting in their time. Individuals in daily conversation come up with great business ideas all the time; but having the power to see the idea grow and expand is a whole extra matter. Read on to learn more.

See It

- Battle the world and all the individuals who want something from you and keep a little picture of your entrepreneurial idea in the front of your mind at all times. If you don't consider it, it won't occur.

- Write all the things individuals say are wrong with the industry where your entrepreneurial idea is centered. Visualize the changes you'd make and write those down also.

- Explore companies that might have a similar idea as yours. Remember no one is stuck in any job. Employees are free to seek out opportunities anyplace as long as they honor their confidentiality agreements.

- Determine whether or not you're the sole owner of the entrepreneurial idea and then tell no one-hire a patent and trademark lawyer and let them do additional research.

- Prepare yourself for other entrepreneurs who will wish to compete with your idea. Don't share data about where, when or how you came up with your entrepreneurial vision.

- Ask the correct questions, be informed, know what you want your future to look like and then make it a truth.

At first sight, the terms entrepreneur and small scale business owner might appear to have the same meaning. They both operate a business and take the profits. The differences between the two are not all of the time clear on the surface, but it has to do with a fundamental attitude of why they operate a business, and the direction that they're going in.

The entrepreneur is known for his ideas. As a matter of fact, he might have many ideas per day; the issue is that they're not all great ideas. A great entrepreneur knows the difference between a great and bad idea, and how to bring great ideas to market, making them into profitable ventures.

To an entrepreneur, it's all about the next move, or where he's going when he's done with what he's doing today. While a small scale business owner might have ideas and vision for his business, the ideas stay inside the realm of what he's easy with and center more on different ways to do the same thing and grow.

A small scale business owner might seek to grow his business, but it might be more through hiring additional staff, or opening a new location. Naturally, there's risk associated with any growth, but the business owner's risk is more limited when he considers expansion; he's frequently doing more of the same thing that made him successful in the first place.

An entrepreneur frequently moves into completely different fields or business models to seek growth. While this is riskier than an easy expansion, he needs to understand how to manage that risk to minimize the effects of a bad decision. Frequently, both the entrepreneur and small scale business owner make foul decisions because they don't appreciate the risks involved.

 An entrepreneur is driven to improve, both himself and his business models. He looks to amplify his presence into more innovative areas and moving into unfamiliar dominion means that he might have to learn a few things that he didn't expect to learn, or to do a few things that are completely alien to him.

A lot of small scale business owners base their businesses on skills or resources that they already have. While they'll seek to innovate and better themselves and their products or services, most improvement resources are devoted to bettering skills in the current fields.

The bottom line is that a small scale business owner makes his living from supplying a great product or service at a sellable price. The entrepreneur makes his living by supplying ideas.

He provides fresh, innovative ideas that he has the skills and resources to take to market, and turn into fruitful ventures. He might decide to sell these profitable ventures to business owners, and then move on from there, or he might keep operating them, constantly innovating. An entrepreneur isn't defined by the size of the business that they operate.

Chapter 5:
Going Green

Synopsis

While many green start-up companies have stapled their hopes on one of newest clean-energy technologies, a far smaller group of green entrepreneurs is putting their bets on a less known – and debatably brighter – business opportunity in the emergent field of "climate services".

The world's human population has grown so colossal that humanity is, for all pragmatic purposes, living "on the edge" of the planet's carrying-capacity.

As a consequence, little changes in weather patterns – precipitation, average temperatures and so on – may have literally vital significance for the majority of humankind. Global warming is galvanizing changes – mostly little changes – in historical weather patterns in many parts of the world.

The New Wave

"Climate services" encompasses the full spectrum of data and analytic systems created to enhance cognition of near-term variability of atmospheric conditions. This knowledge is crucial for everybody, but for a lot of industry sectors and government planners it's of existential significance. Think about a few numbers:

- o Less than a hundred weather disasters in the USA. resulted in total losses of more than exceeding $700 billion over the past thirty years

- o On the average, 629 individuals have died as a direct result of weather each year since 1999

- o Harmful weather on highways and roads induces roughly 1.5 million accidents, 7,400 deaths, 700,000 injuries and $42 billion in losses each year

- o $4.2 billion is lost every year as a result of weather-related air traffic holds

In a late field of study, the US Government. Joint Global Climate Change Research Institute, which is located at the University of Maryland, projected the affect of global climate change on agricultural yields in Huang-Hai Plain, which is among the most productive agricultural areas of China.

The study feigned changes in agricultural yields as a result of altering precipitation and temperature patterns, finding that crop yields might increase under the higher temperature and precipitation under a lot of climate-change scenarios in this area.

Needless to say, anticipating the weather with greater preciseness would provide prodigious lucrative opportunities. The estimated economic advantages of public weather forecasts is about $31.5 billion every year, compared to the $5.1 billion cost of rendering the data.

Expect both numbers to advance and rise rapidly as weather patterns begin to destabilize under the strain of global climate change. This instability likewise makes meteorology, which is already very hard, immensely more so.

Weather is a classic illustration of a disorderly system. It never exactly duplicates itself. The chaotic nature of weather likewise limits our ability to make precise long-range forecasts.

The physicist Teller estimated that a constellation of satellites supplying continuous atmospheric measurements over a one square km grid worldwide, which is presently cost-prohibitive, would only better long-range forecasts from the current 5 days to more or less 14 days.

Climate-services companies are formulating fresh modeling and observational tools, innovative forecasting products and advanced data dissemination techniques designed to master the mechanics of climate and weather.

For instance, Vaisala, an environmental monitoring and analytics company based in Colorado, has established a suite of next-generation meteorology products and services catering to institutions like insurers and government authorities.

Establishing these advanced models will call for exploitation of the ensemble of modeling more fully to produce quantitative probabilistic forecasts of atmospheric quantities with estimates of uncertainness to generate probabilistic forecasts of the affects and risks of weather calamities.

The daunting scale this work entails has kept the number of lower companies operating in this field reasonably small. Expect that to change over the following few years as the US Government. And other governments scale up investments in the environmental monitoring systems and data infrastructure assets.

Chapter 6:
Why You Must Look For Alternatives

Synopsis

Maybe you've heard of the "three-legged stool". Traditionally, retirement has been conceivable because of this stool. The first leg was employer-funded pension revenue, the second Social Security revenue, and the third leg personal nest egg.

In the past, those 3 revenue sources provided most retirees with sizable financial security. But that won't be the case in the time to come.

Consider This

Leg 1: Employer-funded (defined-benefit) pensions have slumped markedly. As a matter of fact, according to the cutting-edge report from the Pension Benefit Guaranty Corporation (www.pbgc.gov), employer-funded pension accounts peaked at 114,400 in 1985 and have since slumped to lower than about 32,500.

Because these plans got too expensive to fund and administer, and the financial weight would increase quickly as the baby boomers—those born between 1946 and 1964—started retiring, a lot of employers took a pre-emptive step and swapped from employer-funded plans to 401(k) plans where employees chiefly fund their own pensions.

Employers might match their workers' contributions up to a particular limit in these plans, or they might not. That means the pensions of most future retirees will depend upon how much they contribute themselves—and few are contributing enough.

As a matter of fact, the Investment Company Institute (www.ici.org) reported that the average 401(K) account balance as of year-end 2001 was only $43,215; older workers commonly have higher balances, younger workers humbler balances.

Only eleven percent of 401(K) accounts have balances better than $100,000 while forty-five percent have balances less than $10,000. And nearly fifty percent of private sector American workers are not covered by an employer-based plan the least bit.

Leg 2: The old stand-by, Social Security, is in financial jeopardy. As a matter of fact, according to the Social Security Administration's 2002 Summary Report (www.ssa.gov), the sum of money coming in (FICA taxes) will be less than the benefits being disbursed by 2017.

Put differently, if nothing changes, Social Security will be bankrupt. While annual discussions carry on in Congress concerning how to settle this upcoming crisis, nothing has been done to date to amend the inevitable.

Leg 3: That leaves personal nest egg. If more cash was being invested in IRAs and other pension plans, and/or in other mutual fund accounts (taxable or not), this leg wouldn't be as much of a headache.

All the same, the overall savings rate in America is at depression-era levels, and most studies reveal that few individuals are saving anywhere near enough to support themselves through retirement.

Chapter 7:
Take Control

Synopsis

If the future of the three-legged stool seems grim, rest assured that it's going to affect a few more than other people. The reality for all of us is that we will not be able to bet on the federal government and our employers to take care of us in retirement like they're taking care of today's golden agers.

So what can and ought we do? Take charge. If you take charge of your life and begin planning for the future, you'll spend less, save more, and invest the difference with wisdom. That is your solution to retiring young.

The earlier you begin taking charge, the more you'll save and invest and the faster your cash will grow over time—to a level where working becomes optional instead of mandatory.

Additional Points

How do you spend to a lesser extent?

First of all, simplify your life. Most individuals work to support their assets; the more stuff you own the harder you have to work to purchase and maintain those things. Quit trying to keep up with the Joneses and rediscover how the simple things in life—like visiting with acquaintances, reading, walking, and spending select time with your mate and youngsters—can be as enjoyable as your latest high-tech buy.

Choose to live with less so that it doesn't cost so much to live. Pick up a few books at the library on simplifying your life. And while you're there, view the other entertainment available at the library at no cost to you. When you do buy something make sure it is a money making purchase.

Secondly, when you do make purchases, go for less-expensive alternatives in food, apparel, vehicles, and vacations. Find as many free and low-cost activities as you are able to for entertainment. Watch for sales, frequent the clearance racks when apparel shopping, establish spending precedence, don't purchase unnecessary items if you can't afford to pay for them with cash, research buys and comparison shop to get the best value, and capitalize on off-peak discounts for travel/recreation, movies, dining out, and purchasing seasonal items.

How do you save more?

This ought to be pretty obvious after what you just read. Spend to a lesser extent and invest the difference between what you could have spent and what you really spent. Think about bonuses, raises, tax refunds, and gifts as "additional" money and invest them for your future. Capitalize on your employer-sponsored retirement account—like a 401(k)—where the cash is taken directly from your paycheck (before you see it so you don't miss it) and invested in mutual funds or some early asset.

You are able to likewise ask your employer or bank to send a check or direct-deposit money from your payroll check into a non-retirement mutual fund account. This is a "forced-savings" arrangement that may work well for individuals who are less-disciplined in saving and investing on their own.

Over the past seventy-seven years, the stock market has far surpassed the performance of the other two major asset classes—bonds and cash—pulling an average annual return of a little over ten percent. Although there are no future guarantees, based on historical functioning and over long periods of time, those centered on growing net worth will do significantly better in stocks than in bonds or cash. You are able to easily invest via mutual funds to diversify your investments and spread out the risks.

There's no question that the securities market has its ups and downs. But if you wish to grow net worth sufficient for retiring young, and if you plan to invest for the long-run (20 to 30 years or more), there has been no better means in the past of achieving that goal than the securities market or currency trading.

Wrapping Up

Retiring young offers many advantages: freedom to get up each day and do whatever you wish to do, opportunity to quest after hobbies and favored activities that there aren't enough hours in the day or week for now, limitless time to spend with loved ones and acquaintances, and a perpetual vacation rather than 2 or 3 weeks a year.

If that sounds great to you, then it's time to start centering on retiring while you're young, healthy, and motivated to take full advantage of what early retirement has to provide.

Most individuals believe they need to be wealthy to retire young. They don't. Many individuals have retired in their 40s or 50s without being rich; but neither were they poor. The net worth you're going to need will depend upon the lifestyle you wish to live.

And the philosophy is quite easy: if you are able to live on less than most individuals, you are able to likely retire earlier than most individuals. If you wish to retire young, spend less, save more, and invest wisely.

Naturally, those fortunate enough to get a windfall (like an inheritance) or who will get an employer-funded pension, won't need a net worth as high as those not having such benefits. And there's yet another option for those who earn less or haven't managed to save the net worth essential to fully retire. Part-time work during early retirement may still give you far more freedom than you have now while supplying an income stream that may make retiring early possible.

You are able to give yourself the choice—to retire young or to keep working—but only when you plan ahead and build the net worth sufficient to having that option in the future.

You might love your job now, but what about in 10, 15, or even 20 years? Exuberance for your job or career may change dramatically.

And with the number of layoffs we have seen by corporations in preceding years, whether you've a job or not in the future might not be your choice.

So take charge of your life now and prepare yourself for whatever might come. Spend less, save more, and invest wisely. You don't have to work always—if you begin planning today. As a matter of fact, you may even retire young!